I0426264

June 2012

APPRAISED VALUES ON TAX RETURNS

Burdens on Taxpayers Could Be Reduced and Selected Practices Improved

G A O

Accountability ★ Integrity ★ Reliability

GAO-12-608

June 2012

APPRAISED VALUES ON TAX RETURNS

Burdens on Taxpayers Could Be Reduced and Selected Practices Improved

Why GAO Did This Study

Misstated appraisals used to support tax returns have long caused concern. In 2006, Congress adopted the Pension Protection Act, which changed the criterion for when appraisals are considered to be substantially misstated and created a penalty for improper appraiser practices and qualifications for appraisers with respect to noncash charitable deductions. The Tax Technical Corrections Act of 2007 extended the penalty for misstated appraisals to estate and gift taxes.

Among its objectives, GAO was asked to (1) describe the extent to which individual, estate, and gift tax returns are likely to involve an appraiser and the extent to which IRS audits them; (2) describe how IRS selects returns likely to involve appraisals for compliance examinations, and assess whether the current appraisal threshold is useful; and (3) assess IRS procedures for ensuring that its appraisal experts are qualified.

To accomplish these objectives, GAO analyzed IRS data, reviewed IRS guidance, and interviewed appropriate IRS officials.

What GAO Recommends

GAO recommends that IRS develop a comprehensive quality review program for Art Appraisal Services (AAS) and establish appraisal training requirements specifically for AAS staff. Congress also should consider raising the dollar threshold at which qualified appraisals are required for noncash contributions to reflect inflation. IRS agreed with our recommendations.

View GAO-12-608. For more information, contact James R. White at (202) 512-9110 or whitej@gao.gov.

What GAO Found

Appraisers' most prominent role relative to the three types of tax returns GAO studied is in the valuation of estates. In the most recent years for which GAO had data, appraisers were likely involved in the valuation of property worth from $75 billion to $167 billion reported on estate tax returns in 2009. In contrast, less than $17 billion worth of gifts in 2009 and less than $10 billion in noncash contributions in 2008 likely involved an appraiser. Gift tax returns that likely used appraisers had higher audit rates than gift returns that were unlikely to have appraisers. The use of appraisers was not associated with higher audit rates for estate tax returns and individual returns with noncash contributions.

The Extent to Which Appraisers Are Involved in Different Types of Returns

Type of return	Returns likely to involve an appraiser as a percentage of all returns in that category	Estimated value of property likely to involve an appraiser
Estate tax returns (filed in 2009)	90 percent to 95 percent	$75 billion to $167 billion
Gift tax returns (filed in 2009)	14 percent to 19 percent	$13 billion to $17 billion
Returns with noncash contributions (tax year 2008)	Less than 1 percent	Less than $10 billion

Source: GAO analysis of IRS data.

The Internal Revenue Service's (IRS) procedures for selecting returns to audit do not specifically target noncash contributions or gift or estate tax returns supported by appraisals. Nevertheless, returns with appraisals do get included in the population of audited returns because certain types of returns on which IRS does focus, such as higher-income ones, are also the most likely ones to have noncash charitable contributions that require appraisals. The current appraisal threshold for certain contributions over $5,000 has existed since 1984. The absence of an inflation adjustment over the past 25 years means that many contributors who pay for appraisals would not have needed to do so when the current threshold was first introduced. IRS seldom takes issue with appraisals for noncash contributions. Consequently, there seems to be little risk in Congress raising the $5,000 dollar threshold.

IRS appraisal experts in one division met standards for ensuring that they were qualified. However, art appraisal experts in another division are not subject to either a comprehensive quality review program or continuing education requirements specific to appraising art. The lack of comprehensive quality reviews and mission-specific continuing education requirements could make the art appraisers less effective than they otherwise would be.

Contents

Tables

Figures

Abbreviations

AAS	Art Appraisal Services
AQMS	Appeals Quality Measurement System
CIC	coordinated industry case
EOAD	Examination Operational Automation Database
ERIS	Enforcement Revenue Information System
IC	industry case
IRM	*Internal Revenue Manual*
IRS	Internal Revenue Service
LB&I	Large Business and International Division
OPR	Office of Professional Responsibility
PPA	Pension Protection Act of 2006
SB/SE	Small Business and Self-Employed Division
SOI	Statistics of Income
TTCA	Tax Technical Corrections Act of 2007
USPAP	Uniform Standards of Professional Appraisal Practice

June 5, 2012

The Honorable Max Baucus
Chairman
The Honorable Orrin Hatch
Ranking Member
Committee on Finance
United States Senate

The Honorable Charles Grassley
Ranking Member
Committee on the Judiciary
United States Senate

The tax liabilities of individuals who make noncash charitable donations or who receive inheritances or gifts of property can depend significantly on the valuation of the property. Valuable property such as art, cars, businesses, real estate, and easements, by law must be independently appraised to determine exactly how much the taxpayer should report on a tax return. An appraisal is an opinion about the value of a particular asset at a particular time and is prepared following professionally accepted procedures. If appraisals overvalue the property in the case of charitable donations, or undervalue the property in the case of bequests or gifts, taxpayers may—intentionally or mistakenly—pay less tax than they should. Although the Internal Revenue Service (IRS) has not determined the extent to which appraisals contribute to misreporting, data from an IRS study on taxpayer noncompliance showed a 45 percent error rate on noncash charitable deductions, totaling $4.6 billion in lost revenue. For about every five errors favorable to the taxpayer, one was unfavorable to the taxpayer. In 2005 IRS and the Joint Committee on Taxation identified overvalued donations of conservation easements[1] as a particularly problematic issue. The problem persists. In 2011 the Department of Justice sought and the District Court for the District of Columbia issued an injunction against a company that IRS identified as improperly encouraging taxpayers to seek appraisers who would misvalue

---

[1] A conservation easement represents a contractual agreement between the property owner and a charitable organization receiving the easement to preserve the property.

conservation easement contributions on building façades for noncash charitable deductions.[2]

Congress addressed appraisal-related noncompliance in the Pension Protection Act of 2006 (PPA) and the Tax Technical Corrections Act of 2007 (TTCA). The PPA lowered the thresholds on when IRS should consider appraisals misstated, established a civil penalty for preparing a misstated appraisal, and set a statutory definition on qualifications for appraisers with respect to charitable deductions.[3] TTCA extended the civil penalties for misstated appraisals to estate and gift tax valuations.[4]

Because of your interest in how these laws may have affected tax compliance, you asked us to review IRS's enforcement efforts with respect to appraisals. In this report we (1) describe the extent to which individual, estate, and gift tax returns are likely to involve appraisers' valuations, the extent to which IRS audits such returns, and the extent to which appraiser-specific penalties have been levied; (2) describe how IRS selects and staffs returns likely to involve appraisers that it chooses for examination, how examiners determine whether an appraisal is accurate, and the extent to which IRS uses contractors to provide appraisal expertise, as well as assess the usefulness of the current appraisal reporting threshold; and (3) assess IRS's procedures for ensuring that its appraisal experts are qualified.

To identify the extent to which appraisers' valuations may cause an issue for estate and gift tax returns and for returns of individuals making noncash charitable contributions, we analyzed IRS Statistics of Income (SOI) samples of these three populations of returns for filing years 2007 through 2009 (for estate and gift tax) and tax years 2005 through 2008 (for individual returns with noncash contributions).[5] To identify the rate at

---

[2] United States v. McClain, Civil No. 11-1087 (D.D.C. July 13, 2011) (stipulated order of permanent injunction).

[3] Pub. L. No. 109-280, 120 Stat. 780 (2006). According to the law, qualified appraisers must have an appraisal designation from a recognized appraisal organization or meet education requirements set by the Secretary of the Treasury, regularly perform appraisals, and meet other standards set by the Secretary of the Treasury. IRC §170(f)(11)(E)(ii).

[4] Pub. L. No. 110-172, 121 Stat. 2473 (2007).

[5] See app. I for a detailed description of this analysis. We used different time periods because of differences in the availability of data from SOI.

which IRS audits returns with potential issues caused by appraisers and the amounts of tax adjustments for appraiser-related cases, we had IRS match the cases we analyzed from the SOI sample of taxpayers claiming noncash contributions against examination results data available from the Examination Operational Automation Database (EOAD), which contains information on audit adjustments relating to specific audit issues. Given the limitations of the issue coding in the database, we can reliably report on adjustments relating to noncash contributions but not specifically relating to the appraisal of those contributions. EOAD does not contain data for estate and gift tax audits, so we had IRS match the SOI cases for those taxes to data from the Enforcement Revenue Information System. This process allowed us to reliably determine which returns were audited. We calculated confidence intervals for all of our estimates. To report the number of appraiser penalties, we consulted with the IRS penalties officials who track the penalty created under the PPA.

To describe how IRS selects and staffs appraisal-related examinations, we reviewed IRS staffing and case selection procedures and interviewed IRS officials responsible for examination planning. To gather information on how IRS audits tax returns with appraisals, we identified through our data analysis a random sample of tax year 2008 returns that were likely to involve appraisals and that had been audited by IRS. We then reviewed the examination files for these cases to identify any inconsistencies between stated examination policies in the *Internal Revenue Manual* (IRM) and the recorded activities of examiners. To determine the extent of contractor use for appraisal-related examinations, we reviewed contracting procedures in the IRM and other documentation from IRS. We then compiled data from IRS records detailing the use of contractors. GAO previously has found IRS's system for recording contracts to be unreliable for financial accounting, but the data was still reliable for purposes of this report. To assess how IRS ensures that its appraisal experts are qualified, we identified the types of experts IRS uses and compared IRS hiring, training, and performance quality review procedures with standards that GAO has proffered in the past regarding human capital management. We also interviewed officials responsible for staff performance quality.

We determined for the purposes of this review that the data used were reliable (see app. I for details on our scope and methodology). We conducted this performance audit from October 2010 through June 2012 in accordance with generally accepted government auditing standards. Those standards require that we plan and perform the audit to obtain sufficient, appropriate evidence to provide a reasonable basis for our findings and conclusions based on our audit objectives. We believe that the evidence obtained provides a reasonable basis for our findings and conclusions based on our audit objectives.

Background

The PPA set stricter standards for appraisals and appraiser qualifications, established a penalty on appraisers who prepared appraisals that improperly supported deductions on income taxes, and lowered the threshold for determining certain misstatements of value on certain tax returns.

In terms of noncash charitable contributions, the PPA defined a "qualified appraisal" as one that was conducted in accordance with generally accepted standards by a "qualified appraiser."[6] A "qualified appraiser" is defined as an individual who has earned an appraisal designation from a recognized professional appraiser organization or has met the minimum education and experience requirements set forth in the IRS regulations, and who regularly performs appraisals for compensation.[7] For individuals, noncash charitable contributions are reported on Form 1040, U.S. Individual Tax Return, Schedule A, Itemized Deductions, and contributions of $500 or more must be itemized on Form 8283, Noncash Charitable Contributions. With certain exceptions, taxpayers claiming noncash contribution deductions of items or groups of similar items exceeding $5,000 must obtain qualified appraisals for the donated property, and report those on Form 8283, Section B (see app. II for more detail).[8] The provisions concerning qualified appraisals do not apply to estate or gift taxes. For those taxes IRS simply requires taxpayers to

---

[6] I.R.C. §170(f)(11)(E)(i) and §170(f)(11)(E)(ii). There is no single, universally accepted set of appraisal standards that apply to every situation in which an appraisal might be used, but some professional appraiser associations have adopted standards with similar principles, such as a code of ethics, valuation approaches and methods, and guidelines for developing appraisal reports. One set of standards is the Uniform Standards of Professional Appraisal Practice (USPAP), which an IRS notice on appraisal requirements cites as an example. Among other things, the USPAP set ethics and competency rules, and established standards for the development of appraisals of real property, personal property, and business assets.

[7] The PPA did not specify what constituted a recognized professional organization, but professional associations, such as the American Society of Appraisers and the National Association of Certified Valuation Analysts, provide professional training, certification, and accreditation programs.

[8] The $5,000 threshold was established by Congress in 1984.

GAO-12-608 Appraised Values on Tax Returns

support property values with an appraisal, which could be a written appraisal by a professional appraiser, but does not have to be in every case.[9] Estate taxes are reported on Form 706 and gift taxes on Form 709 (see app. II for more detail on how appraisals may appear on these forms). In general, the higher the appraised value of a noncash charitable contribution, the higher the deduction a taxpayer might claim. Conversely, the lower the appraisal for property reported on gifts and estate taxes returns, the less tax must be paid.

IRS has long had the authority to impose a penalty on a taxpayer for valuation misstatements included on a return, but prior to the PPA, IRS did not have specific authority to impose a penalty on the appraiser who prepared the valuation. The penalty rate has two levels related to the proportion of the misstatement. The PPA changed the thresholds for the two levels and increased the penalty rate for larger misstatements.[10] The act also added an appraiser penalty, which applies to any person who prepared a misstated appraisal and knew or reasonably should have known would be used to support an individual income tax return.[11] In 2007, TTCA made the appraiser penalty applicable for appraisals improperly supporting estate and gift tax returns.

The responsibility for identifying cases with appraisals and staffing examinations on appraisals largely rests with IRS's Small Business and Self-Employed (SB/SE) Division, which handles complex individual returns and gift and estate returns, and its Large Business and International (LB&I) Division, which handles partnership returns with assets greater than $10 million. Examination of appraisals typically will be conducted with field examination techniques.[12] Appraiser penalty cases are audited separately from the taxpayer examination cases in which IRS may have first noticed improper appraisals.

---

[9] In this report we use "appraisal" to mean a valuation made for estate or gift tax purposes by a professional appraiser or a qualified appraisal for purposes of noncash charitable contributions.

[10] For more information on how the thresholds changed under the PPA, see app. II.

[11] The penalty on an appraiser would be the lesser of (1) the greater of $1,000 or 10 percent of the underpayment derived from the misstated appraisal or (2) 125 percent of the gross income received by the appraiser for preparing the appraisal.

[12] A field examination typically involves IRS visiting the taxpayers' place of work or residence.

Appraiser Use Is Most Prominent in Estate Taxes, Is Associated with a Higher Probability of Being Audited for Gift Tax Returns, and Has Led to Six PPA Penalties

Appraisers Play a More Prominent Role in the Reporting of Estate Taxes Than Gift Taxes or Individuals' Noncash Charitable Contributions

We estimated that more than 90 percent of estate tax returns filed in 2009 included assets, deductions, or exclusions of more than $50,000 in categories that IRS officials told us were likely to require the use of an appraiser.[13] In contrast, less than 20 percent of gift tax returns and less than 1 percent for individual returns with noncash charitable contributions were likely to need an appraiser. For estate tax returns, we estimated that the aggregate value of property needing appraisers was at least $75 billion in 2009. This was greater than for gift or individual tax returns (see table 1 and tables 2 through 7 in app. III).

---

[13] When discussing estate and gift taxes, an appraisal is a valuation conducted by a professional and may cover a different set of property than an appraisal for noncash contributions. A more detailed explanation of how we determined what types of property likely involved an appraiser is provided in app. I.

Table 1: Estimated Numbers and Percentages of Tax Returns and Value of Property Likely to Involve an Appraiser

Type of return	Estimated number of tax returns likely to involve an appraiser[a]	Returns likely to involve an appraiser as a percentage of all returns in that category	Estimated value of property likely to involve an appraiser
Estate tax returns (filed in 2009)	30,000 to 32,000	90 to 95 percent	$75 billion to $167 billion
Gift tax returns (filed in 2009)	34,000 to 43,000	14 to 19 percent	$13 billion to $17 billion
Returns with noncash charitable contributions (tax year 2008)	Fewer than 76,000	Less than 1 percent	Less than $10 billion

Source: GAO analysis of IRS data.

Note: Dollar figures have been adjusted for inflation to 2012 dollars using the U.S. GDP deflator.

[a]For estate and gift tax returns we estimated the number of returns with appraisable items of more than $50,000 and $25,000, respectively.

The Likelihood of Audits Is Associated with Appraisals for Gift Tax Returns Being Audited but Not for Other Returns

For returns filed in 2007 through 2009, we found that gift tax filers who were likely to have needed an appraiser were at least twice as likely to have been audited than gift tax filers who were not likely to have needed an appraiser.[14] Conversely, for estate tax returns we found no statistically significant evidence that the likely use of an appraiser was associated with a higher probability of being audited. Audit rates for estate tax returns (which ranged from 8.1 percent for returns filed in 2007 to 10.1 percent for those filed in 2009) are typically significantly higher than those for gift tax and individual income tax returns.[15]

For individual income tax returns for tax years 2005 through 2008, we could also not detect any statistically significant differences in audit rates based on the likeliness that a Form 8283 filer required a qualified appraisal.[16] For most years, we found no statistically significant differences between the audit rates for taxpayers who claimed at least $5,000 worth of noncash deductions from Section B of Form 8283 and IRS's reported audit rates for all individual taxpayers, when compared in broad income groups. (For 2007 returns, we found that the audit rate for high-income Section B filers was at least 1 percent higher than the rate

---

[14] See app. III, table 9.

[15] See app. III, table 8.

[16] See app. III, table 10.

for high-income taxpayers in general). We estimated that the rate of individual taxpayer audits that specifically included noncash contributions as an issue was 0.5 percent or less for tax year 2008 but as high as 3.7 percent for tax year 2006.[17] The total amount of upwards adjustments in tax liabilities associated with appraisals issues (and agreed to by taxpayers) was less than $37 million for each year from 2006 to 2008. For 2005 the amount was between $67 million and $91 million.

For most of the years we reviewed, the sizes of our subsamples of audits that specifically identified noncash contributions as being an issue were too small to yield useful information concerning that particular issue's no-change rate.[18] However, in the case of returns filed for tax year 2007 we were able to estimate that the no-change rate for noncash contribution issues was between 72 percent and 97 percent with a 95 percent level of confidence (see app. II, table 12).

IRS officials said the contributions that some individual taxpayers report on their returns are made through partnerships or Subchapter S corporations and that those contributions may be reviewed in audits of those entities rather than in audits of the individuals' returns.[19] We reviewed data for all 121 partnership and S corporation audits involving noncash contributions that were referred to the Engineering Program (Engineering), a group within LB&I that staffs appraisal experts available to examiners for consultation, for assistance in calendar year 2010. We found that in 31 of those cases, the value of the contribution was identified as an audit issue. Separately, IRS officials told us that from 2007 through February 2012, 500 individual tax returns were adjusted as a result of SB/SE audits of deductions relating to conservation easements claimed by these types of entities.

---

[17] See app. III, table 11.

[18] The no-change rate was computed by first estimating (1) the number of cases where noncash contributions were included as an issue to be reviewed and (2) the number of those cases where an adjustment was made to the contribution and then dividing (2) by (1).

[19] Partnerships and S corporations are "pass-through" entities, meaning that they are not subject to the corporate income tax. Instead, these entities' income, deductions, and credits are allocated to the partners or shareholders.

As of March 2012, IRS Had Levied the PPA Penalty on Appraisers Six Times

The total amount of PPA penalties assessed in the six existing cases where appraiser penalties have been assessed was $159,713, with the penalty amounts ranging from several hundred dollars to tens of thousands of dollars. An IRS official said that the agency has not abated any of the penalties.[20]

IRS provided several reasons for the first PPA penalties not being levied until several years after enactment. First, given that the PPA penalties apply to appraisals accompanying returns filed after August 17, 2006, IRS officials said that they estimated that returns containing appraisals that could be subject to the penalty would not enter the audit stream for a few years. Therefore, IRS targeted 2009 to issue guidance and make computer system changes. IRS posted a notice about the legislation in 2006 and on August 18, 2009, issued an interim guidance memorandum as initial instructions for examiners on the application of the appraiser penalty. This guidance, which was developed by SB/SE and accepted by the other divisions of IRS, included procedures to make the penalty accessible by examiners and deliver the appropriate appraiser penalty assessment notices to appraisers.[21] Second, IRS officials said that they had to create the computer infrastructure for examiners to apply and record penalties, draft and approve the form letters to be sent out to those assessed the penalty, and prepare the guidance for IRS examiners in the time between the PPA's passage and the issuance of final guidance on the appraiser penalty. A third factor IRS cited was that its examiners typically conclude a case against a taxpayer before pursuing a case against the appraiser. Figure 1 shows the sequence of events from passage of the PPA to the establishment of formal guidance for examiners in the IRM.

---

[20] An "abatement" is an IRS decision to cancel or annul a tax assessment or penalty.

[21] IRS guidance also instructs examiners who levy the PPA penalty to alert IRS's Office of Professional Responsibility (OPR) about willful violations of the incorrect appraisals provision of PPA. OPR has the authority to impose disciplinary sanctions, such as practitioner disbarment and disqualification, against professionals who practice before IRS, including appraisers, as described in Circular 230, the IRS publication that documents the regulations that professionals must follow to represent taxpayers before IRS.

Figure 1: Events in IRS Development of Appraiser Penalty Guidance, Calendar Years 2006 to 2010

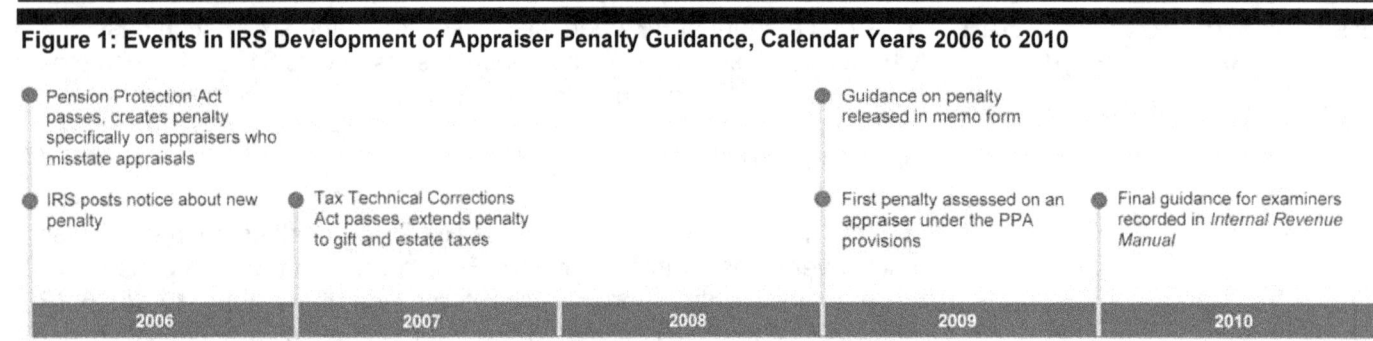

Source: GAO analysis of IRS documentation and public laws.

Application of the appraiser penalty may increase as examiners become more familiar with the process of initiating these investigations, according to IRS examination officials. They said that traditionally, examiners have used other penalties to address appraiser noncompliance. Prior to the PPA, IRS could assess penalties on appraisers for promoting abusive tax shelters and aiding and abetting tax noncompliance under other sections of the Internal Revenue Code.[22] IRS officials said that appraisal issues have never been significant in penalty cases compared to other promoter and preparer violations—officials estimated that maybe 10 or 15 out of every 1,000 penalty cases involved appraisals.

---

[22] I.R.C. § 6700; I.R.C. § 6701.

IRS Does Not Target or Staff Examinations Based on Appraisals, but the Current Appraisal Threshold May Impose Unnecessary Burden on Taxpayers

IRS Does Not Choose Returns for Examination nor Does It Staff Those Examinations Based on Appraisals

IRS's case examination planning and guidance for SB/SE and LB&I field exams does not explicitly target appraisals, but current selection methods may lead to cases with appraisals indirectly. Examination planners in both SB/SE and LB&I use database tools, such as the Audit Information Management System and the Examination Returns Control System, to manage cases for examination, but these databases do not contain variables that would enable exam planning or high-level case selection and staffing based specifically on appraisals. Consequently, when choosing returns to audit, IRS does not know whether any particular return has a related appraisal. For similar reasons, gift and estate returns also are not targeted for specific appraisal issues.

Similarly, IRS does not staff examinations based on appraisals. The examiners who lead these teams are generalists and do not necessarily have specific expertise relating to appraisal techniques. The presence of an appraisal as a potential audit issue does not affect how IRS assigns these generalists to specific cases.

Individual noncash contributions, gift, and estate tax returns with appraisals all may be selected for examination indirectly because of characteristics that are correlated with appraisals. For example, SB/SE field audit priorities focus on high wealth individuals, who are more likely to make the kinds of large noncash contributions, give large gifts, or have large estates that would include items requiring appraisals. In tax year 2008 individuals with adjusted gross incomes of $200,000 or more accounted for over 75 percent of the noncash contributions of real estate, easements, art, and collectibles reported on Forms 8283, even though they represented less than 15 percent of individuals filing that form. Other SB/SE priorities that may indirectly involve appraisals include abusive transactions and special examination projects. Like SB/SE, LB&I does not select cases based on the inclusion of appraisals. LB&I devotes resources to priorities set in annual examination plans and then allocates the remaining available staff to other work.

IRS has targeted noncash contributions for audits, which could include reviews of appraisals, but the targeting is not based on appraisals. IRS selects a portion of its examination inventory using a computerized scoring system called the Discriminant Index Function. Within this system, the presence of unusual, large, or questionable contributions is one of numerous factors that can increase the probability that a return will be selected for audit. IRS also has a matching program that compares Form 8283 with Form 8282, which includes the amounts donee organizations report to have received when they dispose of contributed assets. Mismatches between these returns can lead to an examination.[23]
In addition, one of IRS's past special examination projects specifically targeted deductions relating to façade easements in SB/SE's North Atlantic office, which could have involved reviews of appraisals on the easements' values. The project, which ran from 2008 to 2010, covered 152 tax returns. As of April 2012, IRS said it has closed 60 cases with an average recommended adjustment per return of $252,067.[24]

Examiners May Determine Whether Appraisals Are Accurate in the Process of Reviewing Returns, but the Current Threshold May Be Outdated

Although IRS does not select returns for examination based on appraisals, IRS case-review guidance may lead examiners to detect appraisal issues once a return has been selected for review for other reasons. Different guidance applies to examiners reviewing individual, estate, and gift returns.

---

[23] Donees disposing of contributed assets within three years of the date of receipt must report contributions on Form 8282, with some exceptions, such as amounts received that are less than $500. IRS transcribes Form 8282 annually and electronically matches the amounts reported on the form with the total noncash contribution amounts that taxpayers report on Forms 1040, Schedule A. If there is a potential tax discrepancy of a certain amount the return is classified for potential examination. The classifier manually compares each Form 8282 with the corresponding Form 8283 to further audit the discrepancy and identify the returns with issues that merit a full examination.

[24] The figures cited here refer only to the returns chosen as part of the special project; IRS has audited other returns with façade and conservation easement issues. From 2007 through February 2012, SB/SE, alone, closed examinations on 3,384 returns reflecting deductions relating to conservation easements, which could involve reviews of appraisals.

| Noncash Charitable Contributions on Individual Returns | The guidance focuses examiner attention on a number of issues involving appraisals and related issues, including |

The guidance focuses examiner attention on a number of issues involving appraisals and related issues, including

- checking that taxpayers obtained qualified appraisals, if required;
- verifying that the appraised values of noncash contributions exceeding $5,000 are listed in Form 8283, Section B;
- ensuring that taxpayers attach qualified appraisals for certain assets, such as easements registered in historic districts;
- auditing elements of noncash contributions that seem questionable, such as missing, incomplete or altered forms and documents, and contributions that seem excessively large compared to reported taxpayer income;
- reviewing any large, unusual or questionable items relating to noncash charitable contributions; and
- reviewing the appraisal supporting donations over a certain amount for completeness and issues such as questionable authenticity and appraiser judgment.

IRS officials said that it was up to the judgment of the individual examiner to decide whether the potential additional tax to be gained from investigating appraisals in detail warrants the investment of audit resources. The agency does not require documentation of such judgments when the issue has not initially identified for examination. Our review of 80 examination files from tax year 2008 with $5,000 or more in noncash charitable contributions showed that Forms 8283 were incorrectly filled out in 17 cases but the examiner made no change.[25] In 10 of those cases, the examiner did not leave a record explaining why no further action was taken; therefore, we could not determine whether the examiners made a conscious decision not to follow up on the incorrect Forms 8283. In the other seven cases where the Form 8283 was incorrect and the examiner left a record, the taxpayers supplied additional information during the audit that satisfied the examiners. This shows that taxpayers can be compliant with the appraisal rules even when they do not fill out Form 8283 correctly. We found no obvious incorrectly reported Forms 8283 in the other 63 cases.

Our file review also suggests that, even in cases where examiners do change noncash contribution deductions, few of those changes are due to

---

[25] We define "incorrectly filled out" as the form not having the required signatures from appraisers or donees.

problems with appraisals. As discussed previously, for tax year 2007, examiners made no changes to such deductions in the majority of cases in which noncash contributions were identified as a potential problem to review. Our file review showed that in only a small percentage of the cases in which noncash contributions were changed was the change made due to a problem with an appraisal. These facts suggest that IRS is not finding widespread noncompliance with appraisals for noncash contributions and the potential revenue yield from auditing appraisals of lower-value items is likely to be small. At the same time, the number of taxpayers who are required to pay for appraisals of items with relatively low values (in real, inflation-adjusted terms) has likely increased because the $5,000 threshold has not been changed since Congress set it in 1984. The threshold would be worth more than $11,000 if adjusted to 2012 dollars.

Gift and Estate Returns

Once IRS selects estate and gift returns for examination, classifiers review the returns to identify issues to be audited closely. IRS guidance instructs classifiers to review returns in their entirety, including a review of any appraisals. IRS estate tax return examiners and managers said that estate tax returns can contain voluminous documentation and examiners do not have enough time to go through each appraisal and audit every possible valuation issue. In cases where valuations are an issue for either estate and gift taxes, examiners review the appraisals attached to the schedules selected for examination and make referrals to IRS appraisal experts in LB&I's Engineering Department, as needed. If appraisals are not attached and should be, examiners contact taxpayers to request these. The value of some assets, such as publicly traded stocks, can be determined without complex methodologies, using public market quotations. Examiners also check appraised values using various tools depending on the type of asset. For example, examiners may use "blue books" or other resale guides for personal property, and may use various computer programs that have comparable-sales values for real estate.

Examiners Working on Appraisal Issues Have Access to In-house IRS Appraisal Experts and Outside Contractors for Assistance

IRS employs appraisal experts in two areas, Engineering and Art Appraisal Services (AAS), which provide valuation assistance to examination teams in determining an appraisal's legitimacy. Engineering, as previously mentioned, employs staff appraisers who assist with the examination of complex appraisal issues,[26] and AAS, part of the Appeals Office (Appeals), provides assistance specifically for appraisals of art.

Under current IRS guidance, examiners should refer cases with appraisals above certain thresholds to Engineering and AAS appraisers for assistance.[27] Estate and gift tax examiners must at a minimum consult with Engineering for assistance in determining the accuracy of appraised values for examinations where the focus includes appraisal issues. IRS guidance also encourages examiners to request the assistance of Engineering and AAS experts for cases not requiring mandatory referral, if valuation assistance is appropriate.[28] Our review of examination case files found that examiners made referrals in accordance with the guidance.

---

[26] Engineering employs other types of professional experts; however, for purposes of this report, references to the Engineering Department or engineers refer only to that group's appraisal experts.

[27] IRS policy requires examiners to refer corporate returns with assets worth $10 million or more, and partnership returns with 11 or more partners and gross deductions greater than $1 million to Engineering. IRS policy also says that examiners should refer income tax returns with a valuation issue of $500,000 or more, and estate and gift tax returns with assets valued at $500,000 or more, or with a total tax of $1 million or more, to Engineering. IRS policy requires examiners to refer all cases selected for examination with art valued at $50,000 or more to AAS for review.

[28] AAS also has access to a group of art experts, the Art Advisory Panel, which assists IRS in evaluating taxpayer-submitted art appraisals by reviewing the fair market values for art reported on estate, gift, and individual income tax returns. The panel is composed of prominent art experts, including museum directors, curators, and scholars. The panel makes recommendations on the acceptability of the submitted appraisals, and if it judges them to be unacceptable, makes alternative valuation recommendations for the art pieces. Following review by AAS, the Art Advisory Panel's recommendations on the value of appraised art property may become the position of IRS.

IRS Entered into 23 Outside Contracts for Noncash Contributions, Estate or Gift Tax Examinations Involving Appraisals from 2005 to 2011

In addition to their internal sources of appraisal expertise, IRS examination teams also may seek outside contracts with professional appraisal experts to assist in reviewing taxpayers' property valuations. IRS entered into 23 contracts involving cases of noncash contributions, gift or estate taxes from fiscal years 2005 to 2011. The total amount awarded for the 23 contracts on noncash contributions, gift and estate taxes was $1.1 million, an average of $46,000 per contract. An IRS procurement official said that each contract may cover appraisal services for multiple properties. IRS officials said that it is more economical to hire outside appraisal experts who have expertise with certain types of assets, such as easements, than to have many in-house experts in highly specialized areas because the appraisal caseload in such areas would not support full-time staff. IRS policy requires examination teams to consider the availability and expertise of in-house appraisers prior to requesting the assistance of outside experts.

IRS Follows Accepted Standards When Hiring Qualified Appraisal Staff, but Gaps Exist in Training and Performance Evaluation for the Art Appraisal Service

In our previous work on human capital management, we listed factors for ensuring high-performance human capital management and ensuring high program quality.[29] Standards from our past work that are relevant to our review of IRS's appraiser qualifications include

- having a process suitable to hire qualified staff to audit appraisals, including specifically requiring appraisal expertise as a qualification;
- formally training and educating its staff to keep up with job duties and individual developmental needs relevant to evaluating or auditing appraisals; and
- ensuring that staff are performing quality work during their examinations of appraisals, including a quality review system that covers appraisal skills and management oversight that evaluates appraisal skills.

Engineering fully followed GAO's three standards for ensuring qualified staff; however, while AAS fully met the hiring standard, it did not meet the other two, creating risk that staff may not be performing quality work.

---

[29] See GAO, *Human Capital: A Self-Assessment Checklist for Agency Leaders*, GAO/OCG-00-14G (Washington, D.C.: Sept. 1, 2000).

GAO-12-608 Appraised Values on Tax Returns

Hiring

Engineering: The job description for appraisers in Engineering specifically requires applicants to have valuation and appraisal skills as a qualification, meeting the hiring standard. For example, the description says appraisers must have a "mastery of appraisal principles and concepts needed to serve as a technical authority." The hiring process then works through a combination of automated scoring and personal review suitable for hiring appraisers. Announced appraiser positions follow the Office of Personnel Management category for appraisers, series GS-1171. An automated scoring system called Career Connector assesses applicants' qualifications. IRS then hires from among the qualified applicants.

AAS: The qualifications and hiring process for appraisers for AAS is similar to the procedure used by the Engineering and thus, AAS meets the standard.

Training

Engineering: IRS maintains a formal training program for its Engineering appraisers that starts with new hires and continues with advanced, specialized training, including training on appraisal skills to meet the GAO training standard. The IRM specifies two appraisal organizations—the American Society of Appraisers and the Appraisal Institute—that may acceptable continuing education. LB&I has brought in trainers for some courses and maintains a budget for engineers to seek outside training, as well. Internal engineering training documents also state that engineers may develop a learning plan that includes 40 hours of training every year.

AAS: Appeals requires 24 to 40 hours of continuing education per year for its employees, including its AAS staff, but it does not explicitly identify appraisal skills as a subject for training, preventing it from meeting the standard. Some AAS staff members have attended conferences on visual arts and the law and the American Society of Appraisers National Conference, which appear relevant to their work. However, in contrast to the standard of providing training relevant to specific job duties, the Appeals training guidance does not mention any relevant skills that appraisers must maintain, leaving the possibility that appraisers are not keeping up their skills and not evaluating art appraisals as well as they could. AAS staff have discussed a more specific training program for AAS new hires.

Performance Quality Review and Management Oversight

Engineering: LB&I meets the GAO standard for monitoring performance quality with respect to its engineering group by subjecting its work to a quality review system and exercising management oversight of appraisal skills. LB&I uses an audit quality assurance system as part its LB&I Quality Measurement System. Having such a system enables IRS to improve procedures and issue development.

In LB&I's quality assurance system, engineers are measured on four technical standards. The four technical standards focus on the following subjects

- planning;
- inspecting and fact finding;
- development, proposal, and resolution of issues; and
- workpapers and reports.

Each of the technical standards includes a list of specific criteria. The correct auditing of an appraisal is not specifically covered by the standards. However, to the extent that an examination involved an appraisal, an engineer's work on the case would be covered under these four standards. For example, IRM guidance suggests procedures that an engineer should gather facts. Such a procedure would apply to gathering facts on an appraisal and would be checked during a quality review. To conduct the quality assurance reviews, LB&I randomly selects coordinated industry cases (CIC) and industry cases (IC).[30] The results are reported in quarterly reports. In the first quarter of fiscal year 2011, five CICs covered engineers and three ICs covered engineers. None of the problems directly involved reviews of appraisal issues, but the assessments found problems relating to two of the technical standards on CICs and problems relating to three standards for ICs. On a more routine basis, team managers are required to review case performance, including technical aspects of an engineer's work.

AAS: Appeals operates a case-review program called the Appeals Quality Measurement System (AQMS);[31] however, most of the cases that AAS works are not Appeals cases and are not covered by this system.

---

[30] The CICs cover only those reviews that exceed planned staff days by 25 percent.

[31] AQMS is a system used by Appeals management that randomly selects closed cases to review the quality of Appeals' work in the aggregate, not employee performance.

Therefore, IRS does not meet the GAO quality review standard with respect to AAS. Given that AAS is involved in only a small percentage of the cases that are appealed, IRS's Director of Tax Policy and Valuation said that she has been considering whether to supplement AQMS's random sample with a periodic, targeted review of AAS cases. She said IRS's goal is to start the reviews in fiscal year 2013. Aside from AQMS, IRS guidance encourages examination offices to provide feedback on AAS's performance that "would be beneficial to the viability of this program." The AAS manager also reviews all cases that AAS completes before they are issued.[32] However, there is no group-wide summation or tracking of these reviews or assurance that AAS staff are performing well specifically in regard to their appraisal work, as stipulated by the standard. Without systematic evaluation, erosion of the quality of AAS's work could occur unobserved.

Conclusions

Appraisers play a large role in the amount of tax reported on estate returns, but have less pronounced effects on gift and individual tax returns. Although IRS does not specifically target tax returns that involve appraisals, the policies and procedures that IRS has in place to audit estate, gift, and individual income tax returns ensures some coverage of returns that do involve appraisals. For example, IRS already gives priority to higher-income individual returns in the examination selection process, and such returns are more likely to have appraisals supporting noncash contributions than the general population of returns.

There are two areas where changes might lead to reduced taxpayer burden or improved agency performance relating to appraisals. First, the fact that the $5,000 threshold at which taxpayers are required to obtain qualified appraisals for noncash contributions has remained unchanged for more than 25 years means that some contributors today must hire appraisers to value property that would not have needed appraisals in the mid-1980s, when the threshold was adopted. The high no-change rate that we found through our data analysis and our file review indicates that IRS examiners find relatively little noncompliance relating to appraisals for noncash contributions. This low rate of detected noncompliance implies that very little revenue is gained by auditing appraisals of assets worth

---

[32] IRS Appeals officials also said that they consider the Art Advisory Panel an additional layer of quality review, as the panel reviews AAS work.

less than $10,000. Consequently, there seems to be little risk in adjusting the threshold for price inflation to better reflect the level Congress initially believed was appropriate to deter noncompliance. This adjustment would reduce the compliance burdens for contributors of such property and, if similar adjustments were made periodically in the future, would serve to maintain consistent treatment of taxpayers over time. Second, the lack of appraisal training requirements for AAS appraisers and the lack of a comprehensive quality control process for AAS cases put the quality of potentially high-value appraisal cases involving art at risk.

Recommendations for Executive Action

To better ensure the quality of IRS's examination of appraisal issues, the Commissioner of Internal Revenue should take the following two actions:

- ensure that a more comprehensive quality review system for work performed by AAS staff is implemented and
- develop more specific and documented appraisal training requirements for AAS staff, as LB&I has done for engineers.

Matter for Congressional Consideration

To reduce the compliance burden on taxpayers making noncash contributions, Congress should consider raising the threshold at which taxpayers are required to have qualified appraisals for a particular contribution. Raising the threshold and giving IRS the authority to adjust this value for inflation in the future would maintain the consistent treatment of taxpayers over time.

Agency Comments

We requested written comments from the Commissioner of Internal Revenue and received a letter from the IRS Deputy Commissioner for Services and Enforcement on June 1, 2012 (which is reprinted in app. IV). IRS agreed with our recommendations. First, it agreed that a more comprehensive quality review process is appropriate for AAS, adding that IRS's goal is to supplement AQMS's random sample with a periodic, targeted review of AAS cases starting in fiscal year 2013. Additionally, IRS agreed that more specific appraisal training should be provided, adding that it is finalizing a more specific training curriculum for AAS appraisers. IRS also provided technical comments, which we incorporated into our draft.

As agreed with your offices, unless you publicly announce the contents of this report earlier, we plan no further distribution until 30 days from the report date. At that time, we will send copies to interested congressional committees, the Secretary of the Treasury, the Commissioner of Internal Revenue, and other interested parties. In addition, the report also will be available at no charge on the GAO website at http://www.gao.gov.

If you or your staff have any questions about this report, please contact me at (202) 512-9110 or whitej@gao.gov. Contact points for our Offices of Congressional Relations and Public Affairs may be found on the last page of this report. GAO staff who made major contributions to this report are listed in appendix V.

James R. White
Director, Tax Issues
Strategic Issues

Appendix I: Scope and Methodology

This appendix provides further details on the methodologies that we used to estimate (1) the extent to which appraisals are an issue for estate and gift tax returns and for returns of individuals making noncash charitable contributions and (2) the rates at which the Internal Revenue Service (IRS) audits returns with potential appraisal issues. It also explains how we identified cases for our file review and how we obtained data on IRS's use of contractors.

Estate Tax

The purposes of this section are to document (1) how we have placed the various assets, exclusions, and deductions reported on Forms 706 into three groups based on the likeliness that a substantial appraisal was needed to value a particular item and (2) how we identified specific estate tax returns as being likely to have involved a substantial appraisal.[1] Data for this analysis came from the Statistics of Income (SOI) estate tax samples for filing years 2007 through 2009 (the latest years available at the time of our analysis). After identifying these various subgroups of taxpayers, we used their taxpayer identification numbers to extract data from the Enforcement Revenue Information System (ERIS) regarding any examinations they underwent for the tax years included in our scope. We converted all dollar amounts into 2012 dollars by multiplying them by the ratio of the 2012 index value for the gross domestic product (GDP) price deflator over the index value for the applicable year of death.

Identifying Assets, Deductions, and Exclusions Likely to Involve a Substantial Appraisal

IRS technical advisors for estate and gift tax examinations identified the following assets, deductions or exclusions as being likely to involve an appraiser.

- Retirement plans
- Personal residences

---

[1] For purposes of the estate and gift tax components of our analysis, we define "appraisal" to mean any method used to support the value of an asset, exclusion, or deduction on an estate or gift tax return (this definition should not to be confused with the use of "qualified appraisal" in reference to noncash charitable contributions, which has a more specific legal meaning). We then further break down the term "appraisal" supporting an estate or gift tax return into two categories: simple and substantial. A simple appraisal consists of unsophisticated comparisons that would support the value of an asset, exclusion or deduction—such as referring to statements from a financial institution or to a published price for financial assets. A "substantial appraisal" involves a professional or independent expert using specialized knowledge or professional appraisal techniques to support an asset's value.

- Improved real estate
- Undeveloped land
- Real estate partnerships
- Closely held stock
- Farm assets and farm land
- Private equity and hedge funds
- Other limited partnerships
- Other non-corporate businesses
- Art
- Depletable/intangible
- Family limited partnership, tax value
- Conservation easements

The IRS technical advisors identified the following items that are included in the SOI dataset as being unlikely to involve an appraiser.

- Cash
- Publicly traded stock
- Real estate mutual funds
- Federal, state, local, corporate, and foreign bonds and bond funds
- Other mutual funds
- Insurance, face value
- Insurance, policy loans
- Funeral expenses
- Executors', attorneys', and accountants' commissions and fees
- Schedule L and K debts and mortgages

The following categories contain assortments of assets or deductions that cannot be individually identified as being likely or unlikely to involve appraisers.

- Other assets
- Mortgages and notes
- Other expenses and losses
- Bequests to surviving spouse
- Qualified terminable income property
- Charitable bequest deduction

Identifying Returns Likely or Unlikely to Have Had at Least $50,000 in at Least One Category of Assets, Deductions, or Exclusions That Would Have Required the Involvement of an Appraiser

We identified "returns with over $50,000 in any asset, deduction, or exclusion category likely to involve an appraiser" as those cases with more than $50,000 (in absolute value) in any category from the list of property likely to involve an appraiser above. We identified "returns with no more than $50,000 in every asset, deduction, or exclusion category likely to involve an appraiser" as those cases with no more than $50,000 (in absolute value) in any category listed in either the first or third lists of property above.

Determining Taxability and the Buffer before Taxability Begins

We identified taxable estates as those with positive values for net estate tax. We defined the "buffer" before an estate would become taxable as the amount by which total gross estate less exclusion would have to increase or total deductions would have to decrease (holding credits constant) before an estate would become taxable. In other words, if a taxpayer has a buffer of $100,000, it would take some combination of increases in asset valuations or decreases in the value of exclusions and deductions summing to more than $100,000 before any exam adjustments would result in a tax increase.

Extracting Exam Data from ERIS

We asked IRS to extract selected data from the ERIS database for the sample of estate taxpayers we identified from the SOI data. We counted any case that had a match in ERIS as having been audited.

Gift Tax

The methodology that we used for the gift tax is similar to the one that we used above for the estate tax. The principal differences are that, first, we use a lower dollar limit ($25,000 rather than $50,000) in some of our comparisons because the size of the average gift is significantly smaller than the size of the average estate, and, second, we do not distinguish between taxable and nontaxable gift tax returns. (Many gift tax returns are not taxable; however, the amounts reported on these returns can ultimately affect the amounts of tax paid on estate tax returns.) The data used for this analysis come from SOI's sample of gift tax returns filed in 2007 through 2009, the latest available at the time of our analysis. The property and deduction categories recorded from these returns are slightly different from those recorded from the estate tax returns. We converted all dollar amounts into 2012 dollars by multiplying them by the ratio of the 2012 index value for the GDP price deflator over the index value for the applicable gift year.

Identifying Gifts Likely to Involve a Substantial Appraisal

IRS technical advisors for estate and gift tax examinations identified the following gifts as being likely to involve an appraiser.

- Retirement plans
- Personal residence
- Real estate, improved
- Undeveloped land
- Real estate partnerships
- Closely held stock
- Farm assets and farm land
- Private equity and hedge funds
- Other limited partnerships
- Other non-corporate businesses
- Art
- Depletable/intangible

The IRS technical advisors identified the following gifts that are included in the SOI dataset as being unlikely to involve an appraiser.

- Cash
- Publicly traded stock
- Federal, state, local, corporate, and foreign bonds and bond funds
- Real estate mutual funds
- Other mutual funds
- Insurance, face value
- Insurance, policy loans
- Loans on personal residence
- Loans on other real estate
- Futures and commodities
- Annuities
- Nominal gifts

The following categories contain assortments of gifts that cannot be individually identified as being likely or unlikely to involve appraisers.

- Mortgages and notes
- Other assets
- Adjustments
- Gifts to other donees

Noncash Charitable Contributions

To estimate the extent to which appraisals are used to support noncash contributions, we first reviewed IRS requirements for recording appraisals on Form 8283, Noncash Charitable Contributions. Next, we used data from SOI's annual studies of noncash contributions relating to the amounts and types of contributions that taxpayers reported on various parts of Form 8283 from tax years 2005 through 2008 (the latest years available at the time of our analysis) to (1) identify an upper bound for the number of taxpayers who potentially required qualified appraisals to support noncash contribution deductions claimed on Form 1040, Schedule A, Line 17, and (2) determine how many Form 8283 filers we could identify as either being likely to require a qualified appraisal or unlikely to require one. Filtering the SOI data involved the following steps.

Excluding Filers Who Did Not Claim Any Deductions for Donations Reported in Section B of Form 8283

Qualified appraisals are not required for any donations reported in Section A of Form 8283; therefore, we excluded Form 8283 filers who did not report any contributions in Section B of the form. Furthermore, if a taxpayer reports a donation in Section B but does not carry any amount to Schedule A of the Form 1040, the taxpayer is not actually claiming any deduction for that donation. Consequently, we excluded all filers that did not have a positive value for the amount carried from Section B to Schedule A for any donation.

Excluding Certain Additional Taxpayers Who Reported Amounts in Section B but Should Not Have Needed Qualified Appraisals

Taxpayers should not need a qualified appraisal if either of the following two conditions is met: the total amount moved from Section B to Schedule A for all donations is less than or equal to $5,000, or the only type of donation reported in Section B is intellectual property. We removed all such cases.

Classifying the Remaining Form 8283 Filers for Reporting Purposes According to the Likeliness of Their Needing a Qualified Appraisal

SOI assigns each donation reported in Form 8283 Section B to one of 19 different property-type categories. Donations in five of these categories (real estate except conservation easements, land, conservation easements, façade easements, and art and collectibles) need qualified appraisals unless they come from a business's stock in trade, inventory, or property held primarily for sale to customers in the ordinary course of its trade or business. We believe that this exception is not likely to apply to properties in the first four of these five categories.

To identify donations of art and collectibles that potentially could have qualified for the exception, we did the following:

1. For those filers who made a donation in this category, we used data from SOI's 1040 tax files to determine whether they had a Schedule C[2] business in any of the following listed industry: [3]
    *   Art dealers
    *   Independent artists
    *   Jewelry stores
    *   Jewelry, watch, etc., wholesalers
    *   Beverage and tobacco product manufacturing (wineries are included in this category)
    *   Beer, wine, and liquor stores
    *   Beer, wine and distilled spirits wholesalers

2. We assigned any of these filers that had at least one Schedule C in one of these industries a code that indicates that they potentially had an exception.

Donations in two property categories, corporate stock and mutual funds, are excepted from needing qualified appraisals if they have readily available market quotations or are less than $10,000. This exception can also apply to securities, such as bonds, that are reported in the "other securities and investments" category. We had no way of reliably identifying which of the securities in these categories had readily available quotations, so we did not attempt to identify individual donations as being excepted or not. However, within the "securities and other investments" category, we did identify bond donations using the taxpayers' descriptions of their donations on line 5(a) and assigned them a code indicating that they were potentially excepted, which distinguished them from other donations in that category that were not excepted.

---

[2] Individual taxpayers who have income or losses from businesses that they operate or from professions they practice must report the income or loss on Schedule C of Form 1040.

[3] Given that we are concerned only with individual taxpayers, the only types of business inventories relevant to these deductions would be those of sole proprietorships (Schedule C) or partnerships. To the extent that any of the filers in our sample made only excepted contributions of inventories through a partnership our results will overstate the number of taxpayers requiring a qualified appraisal.

Donations in the categories that do not involve securities may qualify for the inventory exceptions, and vehicle donations can be excepted under additional special conditions. Aside from the "other and unknown" category, donations in the nonsecurities categories, taken individually, account for very small shares of the total value of noncash contribution deductions. The "other and unknown" category accounts for about 6 percent to about 9 percent of the total value of deductions, depending on the year. In some of these cases the type of property donated is truly unknown because the description simply indicates that the donation was made by a partnership owned by the taxpayer. The remaining donations are of such variety that it would be difficult to apply the approach that we have set out above for identifying donations that potentially qualified for the inventory exception.

After we completed all of steps described above, we grouped Form 8283 filers into the following categories:

1. Filers who had a donation in *at least one* of the following property categories:
   - Real estate (except conservation easements)
   - Land
   - Conservation easements
   - Façade easements
   - Other securities and investments (excluding donations of bonds)
   - Art and collectibles (excluding donations identified as potentially qualifying for the inventory exception)

2. Filers who had donations *only* in one of the following property categories:
   - Corporate stock
   - Mutual funds
   - Bonds

3. All remaining filers with Section B donations that did not meet the criteria for the first two categories.

Filers in the first category, on average, are more likely to have appraisals than those in the other two categories; filers in the second category, on average, are less likely to have appraisals than those in the other two categories. We converted all dollar amounts into 2012 dollars by multiplying them by the ratio of the 2012 index value for the GDP price deflator over the index value for the applicable tax year.

Obtaining Data on Audit Rates and Audit Issues

We asked IRS to extract selected data from the Examination Operational Automation Database (EOAD) for the sample of taxpayers that SOI had identified as having made noncash contributions. We counted any case that had a match in EOAD as having been audited. We identified cases as having had noncash contributions raised as an audit issue based on the form and line codes plus the Standard Accounting Identification Number recorded in that database. Given the limitations of the issue coding in the database, we can report on adjustments relating to noncash contributions but not specifically relating to the appraisals of those contributions. We identified audits in which noncash contributions were an issue as having been no-change cases if the agreed adjustment amount for that issue was zero. We used the results of our data matching for tax year 2008 to identify the cases for which we requested examination files to review. We reviewed the cases using a data collection instrument at IRS's New Carrollton, Maryland, office.

We conducted this performance audit from October 2010 through June 2012 in accordance with generally accepted government auditing standards. Those standards require that we plan and perform the audit to obtain sufficient, appropriate evidence to provide a reasonable basis for our findings and conclusions based on our audit objectives. We believe that the evidence obtained provides a reasonable basis for our findings and conclusions based on our audit objectives.

Appendix II: Appraisal Reporting Requirements for Noncash Contributions and Gift and Estate Taxes

IRS has established rules and procedures for taxpayers to follow when using appraisals to support noncash charitable contributions, estate, and gift tax claims.

Noncash Charitable Contributions

Within certain conditions, taxpayers must use qualified prepared appraisals to support noncash-contribution deductions on Form 1040, Schedule A. Taxpayers list the total value of noncash contributions on Schedule A, line 17. Taxpayers claiming noncash charitable contributions over $500 must submit Form 8283, Noncash Charitable Contributions, which has two sections. In Section A of the form, taxpayers report noncash contributions that do not require qualified appraisals. Such contributions include items, or groups of similar items,[1] with a claimed deduction of $5,000 or less, and securities of any value with readily available market quotations.[2] For contributions more than $5,000, taxpayers must have an appraisal done and fill out Section B of Form 8283. Exceptions to the $5,000 threshold include

- nonpublicly traded stock of $10,000 or less;
- vehicles if the deduction is limited to gross proceeds from sale;
- intellectual property;
- certain securities considered to have market quotations readily available;
- inventory and property donated by corporations that are "qualified contributions" for the care of the ill or infants; and
- stock in trade, inventory, or property held primarily for sale to customers.

Figure 2 shows the section of Form 8283 where taxpayers provide descriptions and appraised values of donated property valued at more than $5,000. Taxpayers are required to attach the written appraisals to the return only for contributions of art valued at $20,000 or more, any deduction of more than $500,000, contributions of easements on buildings in historic districts, and deductions of more than $500 for clothing and household items not in good use condition. Charitable

---

[1] Similar items are those that fall under the same category or type, such as paintings, coin collections, jewelry, buildings, and nonpublicly traded stocks.

[2] Securities with restrictions, even if they have readily available market quotations, may require qualified appraisals.

organizations that receive contributions listed in Section B of Form 8283 generally must report them to IRS on Form 8282.

Figure 2: Form 8283, Section B, Part I, Reporting Instructions for Noncash Charitable Contributions over $5,000

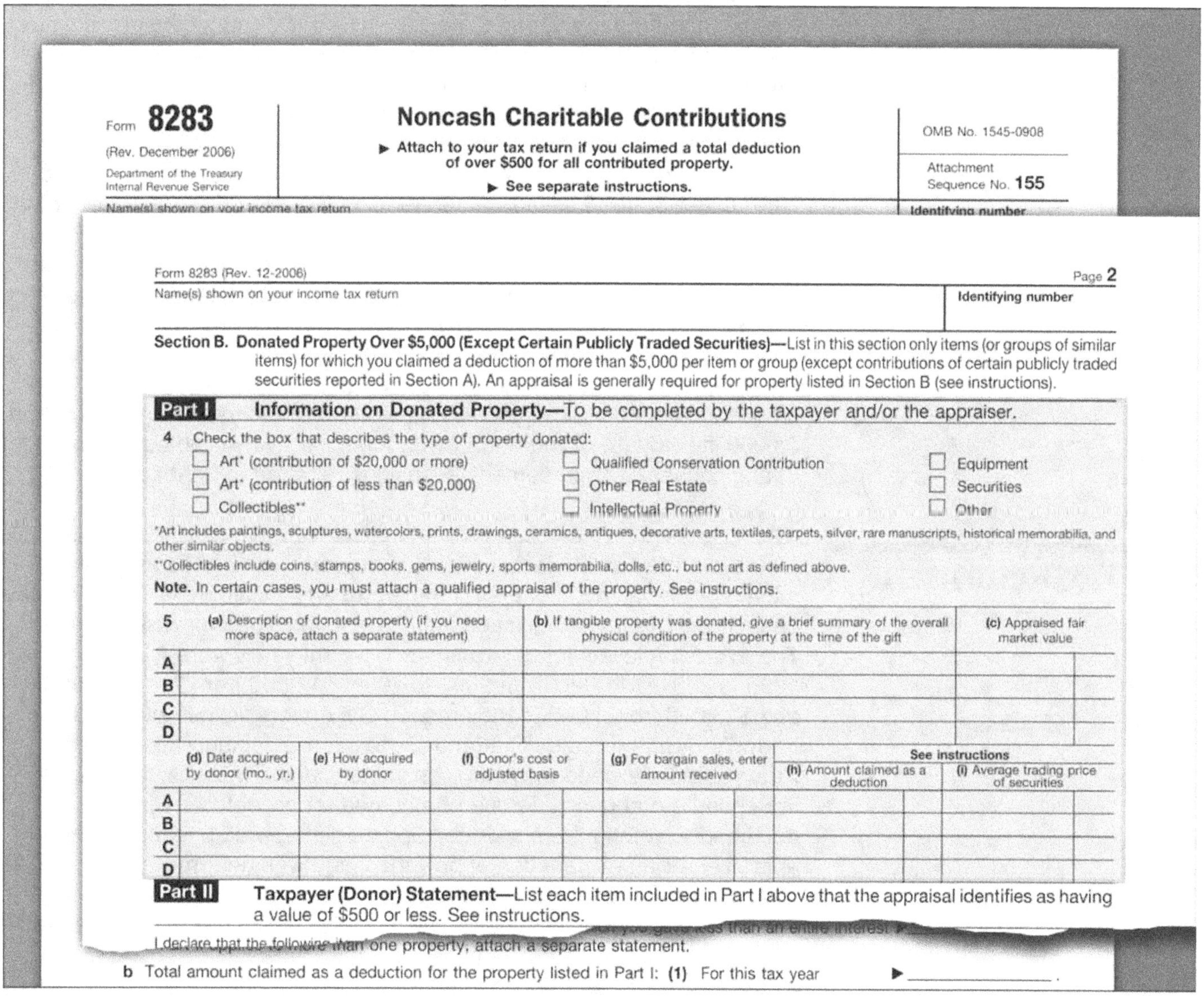

Form **8283** (Rev. December 2006) Department of the Treasury Internal Revenue Service

Noncash Charitable Contributions

▶ Attach to your tax return if you claimed a total deduction of over $500 for all contributed property.

▶ See separate instructions.

OMB No. 1545-0908

Attachment Sequence No. **155**

Name(s) shown on your income tax return | Identifying number

Form 8283 (Rev. 12-2006) Page **2**

Name(s) shown on your income tax return | **Identifying number**

Section B. Donated Property Over $5,000 (Except Certain Publicly Traded Securities)—List in this section only items (or groups of similar items) for which you claimed a deduction of more than $5,000 per item or group (except contributions of certain publicly traded securities reported in Section A). An appraisal is generally required for property listed in Section B (see instructions).

Part I **Information on Donated Property**—To be completed by the taxpayer and/or the appraiser.

4 Check the box that describes the type of property donated:

☐ Art* (contribution of $20,000 or more) ☐ Qualified Conservation Contribution ☐ Equipment

☐ Art* (contribution of less than $20,000) ☐ Other Real Estate ☐ Securities

☐ Collectibles** ☐ Intellectual Property ☐ Other

*Art includes paintings, sculptures, watercolors, prints, drawings, ceramics, antiques, decorative arts, textiles, carpets, silver, rare manuscripts, historical memorabilia, and other similar objects.

**Collectibles include coins, stamps, books, gems, jewelry, sports memorabilia, dolls, etc., but not art as defined above.

Note. In certain cases, you must attach a qualified appraisal of the property. See instructions.

5	(a) Description of donated property (if you need more space, attach a separate statement)	(b) If tangible property was donated, give a brief summary of the overall physical condition of the property at the time of the gift	(c) Appraised fair market value
A			
B			
C			
D			

	(d) Date acquired by donor (mo., yr.)	(e) How acquired by donor	(f) Donor's cost or adjusted basis	(g) For bargain sales, enter amount received	See instructions (h) Amount claimed as a deduction	See instructions (i) Average trading price of securities
A						
B						
C						
D						

Part II **Taxpayer (Donor) Statement**—List each item included in Part I above that the appraisal identifies as having a value of $500 or less. See instructions.

I declare that the following ... than one property, attach a separate statement.

b Total amount claimed as a deduction for the property listed in Part I: **(1)** For this tax year ▶ __________ .

Source: Adapted from IRS Form 8283 Noncash Charitable Contributions.

Estate Tax Returns

IRS requires that taxpayers support the claimed value of property in estate transfers with an appraisal, which could be a written appraisal by a professional appraiser, but does not have to be in every situation. The body of law covering qualified appraisals for noncash charitable contributions does not apply to estate or gift taxes. Taxpayers may owe taxes on the property of an estate transferred at death, if the gross value of the estate exceeds annually established exclusion levels. The exclusion levels for the estates of those who died in certain recent years were $1.5 million for 2004 to 2005, $2 million for 2006 to 2008, $3.5 million for 2009, and $5 million for 2010 to 2012. Following taxpayers' deaths, appointed estate executors file estate returns on Form 706, United States Estate (and Generation-Skipping Transfer) Tax Return if the estate is worth more than the annual exclusion. Appointed executors must include explanation or documentation detailing how the value of estate property was determined. Written appraisals prepared by professional appraisers are one of the acceptable valuation methods, and appropriate documentation will vary depending on the type of asset. However, written appraisals are required to support the value of real property claimed in Schedule A-1, artwork or collectibles worth more than $3,000 individually or more than $10,000 collectively claimed in Schedule F, and conservation easement exclusions reported in Schedule U.

Gift Tax Returns

Taxpayers may be subject to taxes on property transferred as gifts and must provide valuation support for the property's claimed value. Gifts may be taxable if their value exceeds annually established exclusion values. The exclusion levels for gift transfers in recent years were $10,000 from 1998 to 2001, $11,000 from 2002 to 2005, $12,000 from 2006 to 2008, and $13,000 from 2009 to the present. Gift donors file gift returns on Form 709, United States Gift (and Generation-Skipping Transfer) Tax Return, if gifts exceed the exclusion value. Donors must list taxable gifts in Schedule A and include one of a number of acceptable valuation documents, among them a written appraisal prepared by a professional appraiser, or an explanation of how the value was determined. For calendar year 2007, IRS recorded 257,485 donors who transferred $45.2 billion in gifts. Less than 4 percent of all gift returns were taxable, accounting for $2.8 billion in gift taxes. Three types of assets—cash, stock, and real estate—accounted for 87 percent of all gifts.

Penalty Thresholds and Valuation Misstatements

For noncash charitable contributions, the Pension Protection Act (PPA) of 2006 lowered the threshold for substantial valuation misstatements from 200 percent of the correct valuation to 150 percent. Substantial valuation misstatements subject the taxpayer to a penalty equal to 20 percent of the underpayment attributable to the misstatement. For estate and gift property, PPA increased the threshold for substantial valuation understatements from 50 percent to 65 percent. Gross valuation misstatements on any return are subject to an increased penalty equal to 40 percent of the portion of the underpayment attributable to the misstatement. For noncash charitable contributions, PPA lowered the threshold for gross valuation misstatement from 400 percent of the correct valuation to 200 percent. For estate or gift property, PPA raised the threshold for gross valuation understatements from 25 percent to 40 percent of the supported value.

Tables 2 through 12 contain data on appraisal usage and IRS's appraisal enforcement.

Table 2: Number of Estate Tax Returns Filed in 2007 through 2009, by Likeliness of Having a Valuation Done by an Appraiser

In thousands

	Estimate	Lower bound of 95 percent confidence interval	Upper bound of 95 percent confidence interval
Estate tax returns filed in 2009[a]			
Returns with over $50,000 in any asset, deduction, or exclusion category likely to involve an appraiser	30.5	30.2	30.8
Returns with no more than $50,000 in every asset, deduction, or exclusion category likely to involve an appraiser	0.9	0.7	1.2
Returns that could not be classified into either of the preceding groups	0.8	0.6	1.0
Estate tax returns filed in 2008			
Returns with over $50,000 in any asset, deduction, or exclusion category likely to involve an appraiser	34.8	34.6	35.1
Returns with no more than $50,000 in every asset, deduction, or exclusion category likely to involve an appraiser	1.0	0.9	1.2
Returns that could not be classified into either of the preceding groups	1.2	1.0	1.4
Estate tax returns filed in 2007			
Returns with over $50,000 in any asset, deduction, or exclusion category likely to involve an appraiser	34.0	33.7	34.3
Returns with no more than $50,000 in every asset, deduction, or exclusion category likely to involve an appraiser	1.4	1.2	1.6
Returns that could not be classified into either of the preceding groups	1.4	1.2	1.6

Source: GAO analysis of IRS data.

[a]IRS reports that 33,515 estate tax returns were filed in 2009; 38,354 in 2008; and 38,000 in 2007.

Table 3: Absolute Value of Assets, Deductions, and Exclusions Reported on Estate Tax returns, by Likeliness of Having a Valuation Done by an Appraiser

Dollars in billions

	Estimate	Lower bound of 95 percent confidence interval	Upper bound of 95 percent confidence interval
All items reported in 2009	**$257.0**	**$255.0**	**$259.0**
Items likely to involve an appraiser	76.8	75.6	78.1
Items unlikely to involve an appraiser	93.2	92.0	94.5
Items for which appraiser involvement is indeterminable	86.9	85.2	88.5
All items reported in 2008	**$294.3**	**$292.6**	**$296.1**
Items likely to involve an appraiser	87.0	85.8	88.1
Items unlikely to involve an appraiser	109.7	108.6	110.8
Items for which appraiser involvement is indeterminable	97.7	96.3	99.1
All items reported in 2007	**$278.4**	**$276.6**	**$280.2**
Items likely to involve an appraiser	83.0	81.8	84.2
Items unlikely to involve an appraiser	104.8	103.6	106.0
Items for which appraiser involvement is indeterminable	90.6	89.1	92.1

Source: GAO analysis of IRS data.

Note: Dollar figures have been adjusted for inflation to 2012 dollars using the U.S. GDP deflator. Detail may not sum to total because of rounding.

Table 4: Number of Gift Tax Returns Filed in 2007 through 2009, by Likeliness of Having a Valuation Done by an Appraiser

In thousands

	Estimate	Lower bound of 95 percent confidence interval	Upper bound of 95 percent confidence interval
Gift tax returns filed in 2009[a]			
Returns with over $25,000 in any gift, deduction, or exclusion category likely to involve an appraiser	38.2	34.2	42.2
Returns with no more than $25,000 in any gift, deduction, or exclusion category likely to involve an appraiser	196.3	196.0	196.5
Returns that could not be classified into either of the preceding groups	0.2	0.1	0.5
Gift tax returns filed in 2008			
Returns with over $25,000 in any gift, deduction, or exclusion category likely to involve an appraiser	43.7	37.3	50.0
Returns with no more than $25,000 in any gift, deduction, or exclusion category likely to involve an appraiser	213.3	212.9	213.5
Returns that could not be classified into either of the preceding groups	0.6	0.3	0.9
Gift tax returns filed in 2007			
Returns with over $25,000 in any gift, deduction, or exclusion category likely to involve an appraiser	41.2	38.6	43.8
Returns with no more than $25,000 in any gift, deduction, or exclusion category likely to involve an appraiser	201.7	201.2	202.1
Returns that could not be classified into either of the preceding groups	0.8	0.4	1.3

Source: GAO analysis of IRS data.

[a]IRS reports that 234,714 gift tax returns were filed in 2009; 257,485 in 2008; and 243,686 in 2007.

Table 5: Absolute Value of Assets, Deductions, and Exclusions Reported on Gift Tax Returns, by Likeliness of Having a Valuation Done by an Appraiser

Dollars in billions

	Estimate	Lower bound of 95 percent confidence interval	Upper bound of 95 percent confidence interval
All items reported in 2009	**$40.0**	**$39.4**	**$40.5**
Items likely to involve an appraiser	14.0	13.4	14.7
Items unlikely to involve an appraiser	24.7	24.0	25.3
Items for which appraiser involvement is indeterminable	1.3	1.1	1.4
All items reported in 2008	**$45.1**	**$44.3**	**$45.8**
Items likely to involve an appraiser	15.0	14.3	15.7
Items unlikely to involve an appraiser	29.2	28.4	30.0
Items for which appraiser involvement is indeterminable	0.9	0.8	1.0
All items reported in 2007	**$38.9**	**$38.5**	**$39.3**
Items likely to involve an appraiser	14.0	13.5	14.5
Items unlikely to involve an appraiser	24.2	23.7	24.7
Items for which appraiser involvement is indeterminable	0.7	0.6	0.8

Source: GAO analysis of IRS data.

Note: Dollar figures have been adjusted for inflation to 2012 dollars using the U.S. GDP deflator. Detail may not sum to total because of rounding.

Table 6: Number of Taxpayers Reporting Amounts in Section B of Form 8283 in 2005 through 2008, by Likeliness of Needing a Qualified Appraisal

In thousands

	Estimate	Lower bound of 95 percent confidence interval	Upper bound of 95 percent confidence interval
All 2008 returns with more than $5,000 in deductions for noncash contributions carried from Section B of Form 8283	**76.0**	**76.0**	**76.0**
Returns identifiable as likely to involve a qualified appraisal	21.9	16.2	27.6
Returns identifiable as unlikely to involve a qualified appraisal	5.9	3.5	9.3
Returns whose likeliness could not be determined	48.2	37.4	58.9
All 2007 returns with more than $5,000 in deductions for noncash contributions carried from Section B of Form 8283	**72.7**	**72.6**	**7.27**
Returns identifiable as likely to involve a qualified appraisal	19.4	15.1	23.8
Returns identifiable as unlikely to involve a qualified appraisal	12.0	8.4	16.2
Returns whose likeliness could not be determined	41.3	31.9	50.6
All 2006 returns with more than $5,000 in deductions for noncash contributions carried from Section B of Form 8283	**73.5**	**73.5**	**73.5**
Returns identifiable as likely to involve a qualified appraisal	24.8	18.3	31.2
Returns identifiable as unlikely to involve a qualified appraisal	7.0	5.3	9.1
Returns whose likeliness could not be determined	41.8	32.5	51.1
All 2005 returns with more than $5,000 in deductions for noncash contributions carried from Section B of Form 8283	**56.9**	**56.8**	**56.9**
Returns identifiable as likely to involve a qualified appraisal	22.4	17.4	27.4
Returns identifiable as unlikely to involve a qualified appraisal	7.4	5.4	9.8
Returns whose likeliness could not be determined	27.0	19.9	34.2

Source: GAO analysis of IRS data.

Note: Detail may not sum to total because of rounding.

Table 7: Value of Deductions Reported in Section B of Form 8283 in 2005 through 2008, by Likeliness of Taxpayer Needing at Least One Qualified Appraisal

Dollars in billions

	Estimate	Lower bound of 95 percent confidence interval	Upper bound of 95 percent confidence interval
Amounts reported on all 2008 returns with more than $5,000 in deductions for noncash contributions carried from Section B of Form 8283	**$8.8**	**$7.8**	**$9.9**
Returns identifiable as likely to involve a qualified appraisal	6.3	5.3	7.4
Returns identifiable as unlikely to involve a qualified appraisal	1.0	0.9	1.1
Returns whose likeliness could not be determined	1.5	1.3	1.7
Amounts reported on all 2007 returns with more than $5,000 in deductions for noncash contributions carried from Section B of Form 8283	**$14.6**	**$10.4**	**$18.7**
Returns identifiable as likely to involve a qualified appraisal	10.6	6.8	14.3
Returns identifiable as unlikely to involve a qualified appraisal	1.7	1.5	1.8
Returns whose likeliness could not be determined	2.4	0.6	4.1
Amounts reported on all 2006 returns with more than $5,000 in deductions for noncash contributions carried from section B of form 8283	**$12.6**	**$11.8**	**$13.4**
Returns identifiable as likely to involve a qualified appraisal	8.4	7.6	9.1
Returns identifiable as unlikely to involve a qualified appraisal	2.9	2.8	3.1
Returns whose likeliness could not be determined	1.3	1.1	1.5
Amounts reported on all 2005 returns with more than $5,000 in deductions for noncash contributions carried from section B of form 8283	**$11.6**	**$10.0**	**$13.1**
Returns identifiable as likely to involve a qualified appraisal	9.0	7.5	10.6
Returns identifiable as unlikely to involve a qualified appraisal	1.2	1.0	1.3
Returns whose likeliness could not be determined	1.4	1.1	1.7

Source: GAO analysis of IRS data.

Note: Dollar figures have been adjusted for inflation to 2012 dollars using the U.S. GDP deflator. Detail may not sum to total because of rounding.

Table 8: Audit Rates for Estate Tax Returns Filed in 2007 through 2009, by Likeliness of Having a Valuation Done by an Appraiser

Percentages

	Estimate	Lower bound of 95 percent confidence interval	Upper bound of 95 percent confidence interval
All returns filed in 2009[a]			
Returns with over $50,000 in any asset, deduction, or exclusion category likely to involve an appraiser	10.9	9.9	12.0
Returns with no more than $50,000 in every category likely to involve an appraiser	19.0	10.9	29.7
All taxable or near taxable returns	11.2	10.2	12.3
All returns with estate values more than $100,000 below the taxable level	0.5	0.1	13.2
Taxable or near taxable returns with over $50,000 in any category likely to involve an appraiser	11.0	9.9	12.1
All returns filed in 2008			
Returns with over $50,000 in any asset, deduction, or exclusion category likely to involve an appraiser	10.6	9.9	11.3
Returns with no more than $50,000 in every category likely to involve an appraiser	11.9	7.5	17.6
All taxable or near taxable returns	10.8	10.0	11.5
All returns with estate values more than $100,000 below the taxable level	0.5	0.0	3.8
Taxable or near taxable returns with over $50,000 in any category likely to involve an appraiser	10.8	10.1	11.6
All returns filed in 2007			
Returns with over $50,000 in any asset, deduction, or exclusion category likely to involve an appraiser	7.6	7.0	8.2
Returns with no more than $50,000 in every category likely to involve an appraiser	5.9	2.7	11.0
All taxable or near taxable returns	8.2	7.5	8.9
All returns with estate values more than $100,000 below the taxable level	0.9	0.3	1.9
Taxable or near taxable returns with over $50,000 in any category likely to involve an appraiser	8.3	7.6	9.0

Source: GAO analysis of IRS data.

[a]IRS reports that the audit rate for all estate tax returns filed in 2009 was 10.1 percent. The audit rates for 2008 and 2007 were 9.3 and 8.1 percent, respectively.

Table 9: Audit Rates for Gift Tax Returns Filed in 2007 through 2009, by Likeliness of Having a Valuation Done by an Appraiser

Percentages

	Estimate	Lower bound of 95 percent confidence interval	Upper Bound of 95 percent confidence interval
All returns filed in 2009[a]			
Returns with over $25,000 in any gift, deduction, or exclusion category likely to involve an appraiser	0.8	0.5	1.3
Returns with no more than $25,000 in any gift, deduction, or exclusion category likely to involve an appraiser	0.1	0.0	0.2
All returns filed in 2008			
Returns with over $25,000 in any gift, deduction, or exclusion category likely to involve an appraiser	1.3	0.9	1.8
Returns with no more than $25,000 in any gift, deduction, or exclusion category likely to involve an appraiser	0.1	0.0	0.2
All returns filed in 2007			
Returns with over $25,000 in any gift, deduction, or exclusion category likely to involve an appraiser	1.1	0.8	1.6
Returns with no more than $25,000 in any gift, deduction, or exclusion category likely to involve an appraiser	0.2	0.1	0.3

Source: GAO analysis of IRS data.

[a]IRS reports that the audit rate for all gift tax returns filed in 2009 was 0.7 percent. The audit rates for 2008 and 2007 were 0.6 and 0.4 percent, respectively.

Table 10: Audit Rates for Taxpayers Reporting Amounts in Section B of Form 8283 in 2005 through 2008, by Likeliness of Needing a Qualified Appraisal

Percentage

	Estimate	Lower bound of 95 percent confidence interval	Upper bound of 95 percent confidence interval
All 2008 returns with more than $5,000 in deductions for noncash contributions carried from Section B of Form 8283	**1.4**	**0.3**	**3.7**
Returns likely to involve a qualified appraisal	3.2	0.3	12.0
Returns unlikely to involve a qualified appraisal	1.5	0.3	3.9
Returns with adjusted gross income under $200,000	0.3	0.0	1.3
Returns with adjusted gross income above or equal to $200,000	3.5	0.7	9.9
All 2007 returns with more than $5,000 in deductions for noncash contributions carried from Section B of Form 8283	**4.1**	**2.2**	**6.7**
Returns likely to involve a qualified appraisal	4.2	2.0	7.6
Returns unlikely to involve a qualified appraisal	1.7	0.8	3.2
Returns with adjusted gross income under $200,000	0.5	0.0	2.9
Returns with adjusted gross income above or equal to $200,000	7.4	4.1	12.2
All 2006 returns with more than $5,000 in deductions for noncash contributions carried from Section B of Form 8283	**2.8**	**1.4**	**4.9**
Returns likely to involve a qualified appraisal	2.2	1.0	4.0
Returns unlikely to involve a qualified appraisal	7.0	1.0	21.8
Returns with adjusted gross income under $200,000	1.8	0.4	5.1
Returns with adjusted gross income above or equal to $200,000	4.4	2.2	7.8
All 2005 returns with more than $5,000 in deductions for noncash contributions carried from Section B of Form 8283	**2.0**	**1.2**	**3.1**
Returns likely to involve a qualified appraisal	2.4	1.2	4.3
Returns unlikely to involve a qualified appraisal	0.4	0.1	1.3
Returns with adjusted gross income under $200,000	0.5	0.0	2.9
Returns with adjusted gross income above or equal to $200,000	3.4	2.1	5.4

Source: GAO analysis of IRS data.

Table 11: Rates of Audit That Included Noncash Contributions as an Issue for Taxpayers Reporting Amounts in Section B of Form 8283 in 2005 through 2008, by Likeliness of Needing a Qualified Appraisal

Percentages

	Estimate	Lower bound of 95 percent confidence interval	Upper bound of 95 percent confidence interval
All 2008 returns with more than $5,000 in deductions for noncash contributions carried from Section B of Form 8283	**0.2**	**0.1**	**0.5**
Returns likely to involve a qualified appraisal	0.4	0.1	1.3
Returns unlikely to involve a qualified appraisal	0.8	0.0	3.7
All 2007 returns with more than $5,000 in deductions for noncash contributions carried from Section B of Form 8283	**1.2**	**0.6**	**2.1**
Returns likely to involve a qualified appraisal	1.0	0.6	1.7
Returns unlikely to involve a qualified appraisal	1.1	0.3	2.6
All 2006 returns with more than $5,000 in deductions for noncash contributions carried from Section B of Form 8283	**1.5**	**0.4**	**3.7**
Returns likely to involve a qualified appraisal	0.6	0.2	1.3
Returns unlikely to involve a qualified appraisal	4.5	0.2	21.3
All 2005 returns with more than $5,000 in deductions for noncash contributions carried from Section B of Form 8283	**0.7**	**0.3**	**1.3**
Returns likely to involve a qualified appraisal	0.5	0.3	1.0
Returns unlikely to involve a qualified appraisal	0.1	0.0	0.9

Source: GAO analysis of IRS data.

Table 12: No-Change Rates for Audit That Included Noncash Contributions as an Issue for Taxpayers Reporting Amounts in Section B of Form 8283 in 2005 through 2008, by Likeliness of Needing a Qualified Appraisal

Percentages

	Estimate	Lower bound of 95 percent confidence interval	Upper bound of 95 percent confidence interval
All 2008 returns with more than $5,000 in deductions for noncash contributions carried from Section B of Form 8283	**72.2**	**20.6**	**98.6**
Returns likely to involve a qualified appraisal	56.2	0.0	98.2
Returns unlikely to involve a qualified appraisal	100.0	60.7	100.0
All 2007 returns with more than $5,000 in deductions for noncash contributions carried from Section B of Form 8283	**88.0**	**72.0**	**96.7**
Returns likely to involve a qualified appraisal	62.1	32.1	86.5
Returns unlikely to involve a qualified appraisal	86.2	59.6	98.1
All 2006 returns with more than $5,000 in deductions for noncash contributions carried from Section B of Form 8283	**37.3**	**3.3**	**86.4**
Returns likely to involve a qualified appraisal	56.6	15.3	91.7
Returns unlikely to involve a qualified appraisal	99.4	58.7	99.8
All 2005 returns with more than $5,000 in deductions for noncash contributions carried from section B of form 8283	**35.8**	**11..5**	**67.1**
Returns likely to involve a qualified appraisal	63.3	46.7	77.9
Returns unlikely to involve a qualified appraisal	100.0	65.2	100.0

Source: GAO analysis of IRS data.

Appendix IV: Comments from the Internal Revenue Service

DEPARTMENT OF THE TREASURY
INTERNAL REVENUE SERVICE
WASHINGTON, D.C. 20224

DEPUTY COMMISSIONER

Mr. James R. White
Director, Tax Issues
Strategic Issues Team
U.S. Government Accountability Office
Washington, DC 20548

Dear Mr. White:

Thank you for the opportunity to review your draft report entitled, "Appraised Values on Tax Returns—Burdens on Taxpayers Could Be Reduced, Selected Practices Improved" (GAO 12-608, Job Code 450869).

We are pleased your report acknowledges that the Service's Engineering staff has complied with the recommendations from your prior audits, such as ensuring its staff is qualified and properly monitors performance quality. We appreciate that your report recognizes that Appeals provides a significant amount of continuing education per year for its employees, including the Art Appraisal Service (AAS) staff. The IRS agrees that a more comprehensive quality review process is appropriate for the AAS staff. We also agree that more specific and documented appraisal training should be provided.

The enclosed response addresses each recommendation separately.

If you have questions, please contact me, or a member of your staff may contact Faris Fink, Commissioner, Small Business/Self-Employed Division at 202-622-0600.

Sincerely,

Steven T. Miller
Deputy Commissioner for Services and Enforcement

Enclosure

Enclosure

**GAO Recommendations and IRS Responses to GAO Draft Report
Appraised Values on Tax Returns: Burdens on Taxpayers Could Be
Reduced, Selected Practices Improved
GAO-12-608**

Recommendation 1: Ensure that a more comprehensive quality review process for
work performed by Art Appraisal Service staff is implemented.

Comments: We agree that a more comprehensive quality review process is
appropriate for AAS. The IRS's Director of Tax Policy and Valuation is taking steps
to supplement Appeals Quality Measurement System's (AQMS) random sample with
a periodic targeted review of AAS cases. IRS's goal is to start the review in fiscal
year 2013.

Recommendation 2: Develop more specific and documented appraisal training
requirements for Art Appraisal Service staff, as Large Business & International has
done for engineers.

Comments: As noted in the report, Appeals provides 40 hours of continuing
education per year for its employees, including its AAS staff, which includes NYU's
Art Law Day, and national conferences of the appraiser societies. However, we are
also finalizing a more specific and documented training curriculum for AAS
appraisers that will address the concerns raised in the report.

Appendix V: GAO Contact and Staff Acknowledgments

GAO Contact	James R. White, (202) 512-9110 or whitej@gao.gov
Staff Acknowledgments	In addition to the contact named above, James Wozny, Assistant Director; Anthony Bova; Michael Brostek; Sara Daleski; Eric Gorman; Suzanne Heimbach; Karen O'Conor; Melanie Papasian; Albert Sim; Sabrina Streagle; Karen Villafana; and William Woods made key contributions to this report.

GAO's Mission	The Government Accountability Office, the audit, evaluation, and investigative arm of Congress, exists to support Congress in meeting its constitutional responsibilities and to help improve the performance and accountability of the federal government for the American people. GAO examines the use of public funds; evaluates federal programs and policies; and provides analyses, recommendations, and other assistance to help Congress make informed oversight, policy, and funding decisions. GAO's commitment to good government is reflected in its core values of accountability, integrity, and reliability.
Obtaining Copies of GAO Reports and Testimony	The fastest and easiest way to obtain copies of GAO documents at no cost is through GAO's website (www.gao.gov). Each weekday afternoon, GAO posts on its website newly released reports, testimony, and correspondence. To have GAO e-mail you a list of newly posted products, go to www.gao.gov and select "E-mail Updates."
Order by Phone	The price of each GAO publication reflects GAO's actual cost of production and distribution and depends on the number of pages in the publication and whether the publication is printed in color or black and white. Pricing and ordering information is posted on GAO's website, http://www.gao.gov/ordering.htm. Place orders by calling (202) 512-6000, toll free (866) 801-7077, or TDD (202) 512-2537. Orders may be paid for using American Express, Discover Card, MasterCard, Visa, check, or money order. Call for additional information.
Connect with GAO	Connect with GAO on Facebook, Flickr, Twitter, and YouTube. Subscribe to our RSS Feeds or E-mail Updates. Listen to our Podcasts. Visit GAO on the web at www.gao.gov.
To Report Fraud, Waste, and Abuse in Federal Programs	Contact: Website: www.gao.gov/fraudnet/fraudnet.htm E-mail: fraudnet@gao.gov Automated answering system: (800) 424-5454 or (202) 512-7470
Congressional Relations	Katherine Siggerud, Managing Director, siggerudk@gao.gov, (202) 512-4400, U.S. Government Accountability Office, 441 G Street NW, Room 7125, Washington, DC 20548
Public Affairs	Chuck Young, Managing Director, youngc1@gao.gov, (202) 512-4800 U.S. Government Accountability Office, 441 G Street NW, Room 7149 Washington, DC 20548

Please Print on Recycled Paper.